Ruth

REDEEMING THE DARKNESS

ANDREA THOM

E

Entrusted Books, an imprint of Write Integrity Press

Ruth: Redeeming the Darkness

Second Edition

© Copyright 2020 Andrea Thom

ISBN: 978-1-951602-06-2

Published by:

*E*ntrusted Books
AN IMPRINT OF
Write Integrity Press
PO Box 702852
Dallas TX 75370

Find out more about author Andrea Thom at her author page at www.WriteIntegrity.com or at her website: https://andreathom.com/

Printed in the United States of America.

Author's Note

You've picked up a Bible study written by an everyday woman just like you – longing to live intentionally, experience joy, and just stay alert most of the time. I'm a wife, mom, a therapist and a writer. The best thing about my family is being fully known yet still loved to bits anyway. As a therapist I get to watch the same Jesus who spoke creation into life at the beginning of time speak life into broken pieces now. As an author I want my life to have Jesus written all over it – grace when I sin, peace in my devastation, hope despite impossibilities. That's why I love God's Word so much – I'm passionate about teaching how biblical wisdom intersects with our everyday lives and sets our emotions on fire for His heart. It's not ourselves that we should pursue but Christ who transforms us as we pursue Him! He's the only One we can trust to offer real hope and redemption for our eternal future and everyday realities.

The process of discovering Ruth's truths has been one of the greatest joys of my life because I discovered fresh perspective through a story that I thought that I already knew. Over the past several months, I have collapsed to my knees in worship and have been surprised by joy while encountering Christ in new ways. I'm eager for you to taste the overwhelming goodness of Jesus in a fresh and relevant way!

Unlike Hollywood which morphs boring, true-life details into show-stopping displays, the masterpiece that awaits us is categorized as History for a reason—its details are true. This book is magnificent because of its breath-taking storyline between a man and a woman, but especially because God sovereignly orchestrated and sealed its story in the scriptural canon, so that we can experience Him as the ultimate lover of our souls. Ruth conveys the love story of Christ coming to redeem His people. Christ is coming for us. So let's bring the real you and me to meet the living Jesus so that He can move in honest places like yours and mine. Ready?

To a renewed spectacle of God's love in our hearts,

Andrea

Contents

Participant Guide

Engaging in Bible study is both a privilege and a discipline. While we are not all called to be scholars and teachers, we are all called to Christ who is the Word. (John 1:1) When we study Scripture, we interact with Christ Himself! Throughout history, Scripture is the primary and most trusted way that Christ reveals Himself to the world. By it, our minds are renewed and our character is transformed. (Rom 12:2)

STUDY GOALS

I pray that participants will:

1) **Grow** in their knowledge of the text by reading study commentary.
2) **Self-discover** truths through Bible analysis. Information is best applied when students interact with the material being studied. Consider how a diver jumps to greater heights when springing from a diving board compared to leaping from the pool deck. In essence, self-discovery 'springs us from a board'. The depths to which we plunge down in application correlate to our investment into the launch. This study invites participants to look up passages, complete small exercises, and reflect individually and as a group on how to apply truth to life.
3) **Apply** gospel-centered truths in a personally relevant way. The ultimate priority of this Bible study is to showcase Christ so that we can worship Him more fully and live with greater freedom in His truth.
4) **Pray** before each session and throughout the study for God to shape you more into the character of Christ.

STUDY DESIGN

Length
Most sessions are four pages, and there are fifteen sessions in total. Extra wide margins are available to write longer answers or additional thoughts.

Questions
Most sessions contain teaching commentary and application questions. The benefit of group discussion is that it can:

- Grow your knowledge more than if you are studying alone.
- Promote intimacy and accountability to finish.
- Evoke questions which drive you into Scripture for clarity

Meditation

Through Scripture God has started a conversation with us, and in meditation we choose to continue it. At the end of each session, you will find a closing prayer to read, or you can pray your own. Try not to skip a time of reflection and prayer at the end of each session.

GROUP DYNAMICS

Some people find Bible study natural and easy, while others struggle. Regardless of your energy, and comfort level, remember that the hard work of Bible training will be worth the intimacy with God that awaits us at the end.

Dedication

It seems fitting to dedicate the first book in this Bible study series to my awesome family—my first joy and purpose. Seeing your faces each morning after writing into the wee hours of the night kept my heart buoyant with laughter and my mind in proper perspective about my priorities. Publishing this series would be nothing without you standing behind me in support and beside me in celebration. I love you all deeply and this work stands on the shoulders of your prayers, understanding, and encouragement.

Session 1
The Dark Backdrop
• Part 1

Welcome to Ruth! I'm so glad that you're here and excited to get started. Before we jump into the more exciting drama, we need to cover some essential history so that we're looking at this text with the proper perspective. While we wade through background and content in this session, we can be looking forward to the beautiful love story that awaits us soon!

Understanding Ruth can be compared to completing a puzzle. Often, the best place to begin is the straight-edge perimeter that forms a type of frame around the main image. In today's session, we'll form the frame by taking a snapshot of the entire book as a whole and begin investigating some background details. In later sessions we'll investigate the specifics of the characters involved and connect them to the background details we already established. By the end of the book the main image of Ruth will come into awesome clarity and offer a satisfying conclusion for both the characters and us as readers.

RUTH BASICS

The book of Ruth is classified as one of the history books within Scripture. Before we launch in, let's take a few moments to orient ourselves to where this story fits within the larger historical timeline …

God created the world, chose the Israelites as His people, taught them about His character, and established practices of religious and civil law. The Israelites moved to Egypt during a famine, but were eventually enslaved by the Egyptian people. God rescued the Israelites from Egyptian slavery and brought them into the land He had promised them—Canaan. Yet because they were continually unfaithful, God kept raising up judges to call them back to repentance.

Ruth's story takes place during this Era of Judges (1150-1300 B.C.) which was a transition period from the reign of the spiritual patriarchs (Abraham, Isaac, Jacob) to the time of the monarchs (Saul, David, Solomon). Ruth is unique in its size and style—it is a small book with only four chapters and is primarily written in dialogue.

The author of Ruth remains unknown, but he must have been someone who lived after David became king because David and his family line are described in Ruth 4:17-22. The book was written to show God's people that even during hard times, God remains sovereignly in control and His loving-kindness toward them will always endure.

THE STAGE

Picture yourself attending the play of Ruth—the curtain opens revealing a set stage. Theatrical backdrops convey a play's mood, time period, and enhance the actors' performance. Similarly, we need to understand the dark backdrop of Ruth to fully appreciate the richness of the story that unfolds within it. Sometimes, a jeweler showcases a diamond by placing a black, velvet cushion behind the jewel in order to emphasize its brilliance when all visual distractions are removed. So it is with Act 1. Ruth is a story about a diamond, and to fully fall in wonder at its piercing shine, we need a history lesson to understand the black backdrop against which the diamond is contrasted.

Enter Darkness.

How can darkness make a welcome entrance onto center stage? Black is hard. Choking. Hollow. Has your life ever absorbed the sting of aching darkness?

Chapter 1 verse 1 describes the three layers of ugly backdrop that orient us to Ruth's spiritually hostile time period: 1) The days when the judges ruled, 2) famine, and 3) the country of Moab.

Read 1:1–5.

So much for a happy opener! The author abruptly wakes us from our quiet-time chairs with jarring despair. Initially, the first five verses reminded me of a typical Shakespearean tragedy that concludes with the entire cast lying dead on stage. Similarly in Ruth, we hardly have the opportunity to acquaint ourselves with the characters before half of them are dead and the other half are weighted down with sorrow. Calamity isn't the end, it's just the beginning! Original Jewish readers would have fully understood the darkness of these opening verses, yet because their importance is less clear to modern audiences, let's investigate them now.

LAYER 1—The Days When the Judges Ruled

The *days of the judges* were a dark time in Israel's history which reflected their spiritual rebellion against God and was characterized by all kinds of godlessness. It was a period of civil unrest, moral decay, unchecked corruption, religious decline, and instability. The book of Judges details Israel's cycle of rebellion which repeatedly results in their enemies overtaking them. It showcases God in His mercy, raising up judges to save them when they'd hit bottom, again and again. It's a depressing book, ending the way it starts—a nation without a king and the people doing *"what was right in his own eyes."* (Judges 21:25) It is within the thick of this despairing era that the book of Ruth is set.

Read Judges 2:10–23, 21:25. Describe three to five characteristics about the days when the Judges ruled in the first box, and list any similarities to your culture in the second box.

The Days of the Judges in Israel

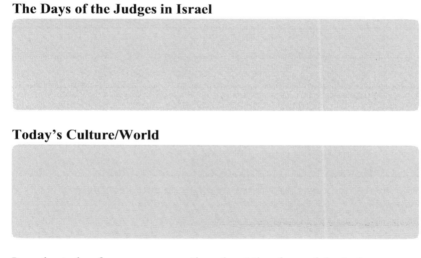

Today's Culture/World

In order to beef up our perspective about the *days of the judges*, we are going to zoom in on one sin that influenced the Israelites' drift into spiritual darkness.

Read Judges 2:10–12a. What did the Israelites fail to do and why is this significant?

The people of Israel were to maintain a holy way of life by cleansing themselves of sinful choices and life patterns. When righteousness *did* mark the lifestyle of the nation, promised blessings from God included the eradication of social problems that were observable to the surrounding nations.

Today, God's people are not isolated to a particular nation or cultural group, but we can still look at so-called Christian communities and see marks of godliness or godlessness. Staying on track with the Lord is not just about avoiding 'the really bad things', but also about prioritizing our focus on the godly things. It is easy to pile onto rafts with fellow Christians but neglect to properly anchor ourselves to the truth. The problem intensifies when we don't even realize that we are quietly drifting down a river heading right over fatal waterfalls! We can be lulled into a false sense of security that we are behaving rightly because we may look around and see that we are in large Christian company.

Judges 2 describes the ship-wrecked Israelite mess being pounded by torrents of consequence that they were reaping collectively. They are gasping for spiritual breath, and fainting for lack of literal food.

Read 2 Timothy 3:1–9. Summarize what a lukewarm church looks like.

Read 2 Timothy 2:10–17. Paul describes the antidote for combatting godlessness within the church. What is his key emphasis?

MEDITATION

Thank You for Your Word that shows us who You are and keeps us on the path of righteousness. Grow our discipline to read it, and may we meet You there as we seek You.

Session 2

The Dark Backdrop

• Part 2

We've already learned that a key characteristic of the *days of the judges* time period was their wishy-washy adherence to God's Word. Today we continue to dissect the dark theatrical backdrop because it significantly impacts the upcoming dialogue and decisions of our key characters.

LAYER 2—Famine

Read Ruth 1:1 and fill in the blank.

"In the day when the Judges ruled, there was a _____."

Ironically, the name *Bethlehem* means 'house of bread'.[1] In the Old Testament, famine can be a consequence given by God when His people turn away from Him. For instance, many years earlier in Elijah's day, God sent a famine of judgment on Israel for worshipping Baal. (1 Kings 16:30–17:1; Lev 26:26; Deut 11:17; 1 Kings 8:35) So, when the original Jewish readers saw the word *famine*, they understood that this was not coincidence, nor natural geographic climate change. Israel was reaping judgment for their sin and begging for relief at the most fundamental level—hunger. They had known better. The outward famine reflected the inner famine of their relationship with God. In short, the consequences of their rebellion were observable.

Think back to where you have struggled. Some women are plagued with guilt for sins that they cannot forget nor forgive. Others shirk responsibility and lay blame elsewhere, never acknowledging that famine has come—at least in part—because of their own sinful choices. Whether the issue is justifying our sin, or shaming ourselves for it, the enemy of our souls wants us stuck in endless cycles of famine—pain and confusion which paralyze us from freedom and joy.

Repeatedly during the *days of the judges*, the Israelites repent and turn back to God with their whole hearts. They weep, mourn, fast, read Scripture aloud, confess, praise, and remember God. It's high drama that keeps repeating! Over and over the Israelites meet their demise and can't get out—so they cry out.

But here's the beautiful part—their desperation for God and acknowledgment of self-defeat qualifies them for renewal and restoration. Similarly, we must let God uncloak our ungodliness and bring us to bare repentance. He longs for us to apply the liberating grace of His Son to our deepest wounds and ugliest sins so that we may enjoy Him more fully and extend the love that we have received toward a broken world.

Personal Reflection

How have you endured famine (physical, emotional, relational) caused by ungodliness?

LAYER 3 - Moabite Neighbors

The Israelites were neighbored by the Moabites, so let's take a better look at these people in order to beef up our perspective on how they impact our story.

Read the passages below and underline what is revealed about the Moabites.

HE LONGS FOR US TO APPLY THE LIBERATING GRACE OF HIS SON TO OUR DEEPEST WOUNDS AND UGLIEST SINS

"So they (Lot's daughters) made their father drink wine that night also. And the younger arose and lay with him, and he did not know when she lay down or when she arose. Thus both the daughters of Lot became pregnant by their father. The firstborn bore a son and called his name Moab. He is the father of the Moabites to this day. The younger also bore a son and called his name Ben-ammi. He is the father of the Ammonites to this day." (Gen 19:35–38)

"While Israel lived in Shittim, the people began to whore with the daughters of Moab. These invited the people to the sacrifices of their gods, and the people ate and bowed down to their gods. So Israel yoked himself to Baal of Peor. And the anger of the Lord was kindled against Israel." (Num 25:1–3)

"And I will bring to an end in Moab, declares the Lord, him who offers sacrifice in the high place and makes offerings to his god." (Jer 48:35)

"No Ammonite or Moabite may enter the assembly of the Lord. Even to the tenth generation, none of them may enter the assembly of the Lord forever, 4 because they did not meet you with bread and with water on the way, when you came out of Egypt, and because they hired against you Balaam the son of Beor from Pethor of Mesopotamia, to curse you." (Deut 23:3–4)

(Optional: See Num 22–24 for more detail)

The Moabites were reputed for being the repeated arch enemies of God and His people. They are the outrageous bad guys in our story because they are rebelliously evil, right from their inception.

Personal Reflection

Describe the *Moabites* in your life—people or behavior that offends you deeply or that you find difficult to forgive.

Here are God's people—rebelling against God, starving because of their disobedience, and neighbored by their arch enemies. This is the ugly stage that verse 1 sets with word props like *judges*, *famine*, and *Moab*. The original Jewish audience would have been aghast upon realizing that Ruth's story unfolds within the middle of this hot mess.

Today, our own lives and culture can parallel these layers. We swim against a current of godless culture which seeks to pull us into Me-centered living. We swim against lukewarm currents hiding within churches that convince us to feel safe in our complacency. We swim against the sinful nature warring within us to disobey when we know better.

Personal Reflection

What current is the most challenging for you to swim against right now?

MEDITATION

Help us discern the ungodly pressures that surround us and pull us away from You. Help us humbly acknowledge where sin lies within us, repent of it, and allow you to realign our hearts to Yours once more.

The Sovereign God

So far, we have introduced some historical context and set the dark background for Ruth's story to unfold within. Today, we move on to examine two characters—Elimelech and Naomi—and investigate the untidy decisions and emotions that accompany their story. God sovereignly reigned over every confusing circumstance and every point of emotional pain, even though logic might have suggested that God had abandoned them.

ELIMILECH - Sovereign In Our Confusion

To *sojourn* means to stay somewhere *temporarily*.[2] Given the temporary nature of sojourning, what irony exists when you compare 1:1 with 1:2b?

Pretend you're Elimelech. Brainstorm reasons to move to Moab or stay.

Reasons to Move to Moab

Reasons to Stay in Bethlehem

To better grasp Elimelech's decision, here's what we know:

- Moab was an enemy of Israel (God's people). Some called Elimelech a traitor because his family left Israel to flee the famine.[3]
- Both of Elimelech's sons married Moabite women, but the Israelites were forbidden to intermarry with Moabites for a specified time period because of the Moabites' repeated rebellion against God.[4]
- Elimelech intended to stay temporarily, but when he died, his family settled for 10 years. (Ruth 1:4)
- Elimelech died in Moab along with his two sons. (Ruth 1:3–5)

However,

- Israel was in spiritual rebellion (i.e. godless *days of the judges*, idol worship), so perhaps it wasn't such a bad idea to leave Israel after all.

- Scholars debate whether it was inappropriate for Elimelech's sons to intermarry with the Moabites—the required time period before being allowed to intermarry may have passed.

- Elimelech's daughters-in-law knew about God because of his family.

- God must have prompted Elimelech's move to generate the story of Ruth.

Elimelech's decision can leave our thoughts untidy, yet it raises a worthwhile discussion point about the complicated choices we make—sometimes we're left scratching our heads in confusion as to whether we made the right one. Whether Elimelech was a backsliding traitor to God and His people, or led by God to relocate for purposes beyond our understanding, in all things God is sovereign and works good for those who love Him and are called according to His purpose. (Rom 8:28) Since Scripture doesn't overtly condemn him for sojourning to Moab, perhaps we shouldn't be too impulsive either. What Scripture assures us is that when our consciences are humble and pure before Him, we can rest in His authority and direction, even when He seems absent, even when we are left confused and second-guessing.[5] Regardless of why our hardships have come, we can trust God who blesses our obedience and has the power to transform our mistakes into something beautiful.

NAOMI – Sovereign When We Feel Forgotten

Read 1:3 and 1:5 again.

The author repeats a similar phrase twice in order to emphasize Naomi's emotional state.

Fill in the blank. "She _____."

Naomi felt utterly *left*.

Look up the meaning of *left* **(in this context) in a dictionary, or describe in your own words how Naomi may have felt in her left state.**

Left: _____.

What a picture Scripture paints of Naomi being devoid of anything but existence! Life is like that. We can grow up naïve and wide-eyed, anticipating that if we behave well and try hard, that life will be fair. Instead, our hearts are pierced through with overwhelming circumstances, and we bleed rivers of sorrow. We've been left. Preserved alive. Emptied.

Have you ever wondered how much of your circumstances are your own fault? Wondered where the mercy and compassion of God have gone even though you've tried to walk with integrity? While some sins reap obvious consequences, other issues in our lives aren't always so clear. As Christians, we have highs and lows, spiritually, emotionally, and every other way. We ride confusing and intense days that do not come packaged in tidy, biblical bows. It's the push and pull of obedience to the Lord. Wins. Losses. Confusion. I-don't-knows. It's all there. And it's overwhelming both in the circumstance itself, and in the struggle of how to process it through a godly perspective. Have you ever felt like this? Overwhelmed? Confused? Guilty? Angry? Exhausted? Bitter? Weepy? Emptied? Feeling left is honest.

> *"Beloved, do not be surprised at the fiery trial when it comes upon you to test you, as though something strange were happening to you. But rejoice insofar as you share Christ's sufferings, that you may also rejoice and be glad when his glory is revealed." (1 Pet 4:12–13)*

> *"For as the heavens are higher than the earth, so are my ways higher than your ways and my thoughts than your thoughts." (Is 55:9)*

> *"Are not two sparrows sold for a penny? And not one of them will fall to the ground apart from your Father. But even the hairs of your head are all numbered." (Matt 10:29–30)*

> *(Optional: Read Hebrews 11.)*

REGARDLESS OF WHY OUR HARDSHIPS HAVE COME, WE CAN TRUST A GOD WHO BLESSES OUR OBEDIENCE AND HAS THE POWER TO TRANSFORM OUR MISTAKES INTO SOMETHING BEAUTIFUL.

Personal Reflection

How do these verses inform your personal experiences of feeling left?

Knowing that harsh emotions have impacted biblical characters can help normalize our experiences and makes us feel less alone. Regardless of the reason behind our feeling 'left', God has allowed its access into our lives. He has appointed it for our good and His glory-filled purposes. But God Himself never leaves us. He crawls into the darkness with us, wrapping His arms tightly around us for the duration of the storm. In this kind of devastation, it is God's divine strength alone that helps us rise and carry on.

Group Discussion

Share a time when you prayed about a decision but wondered whether you chose correctly. How did this experience shape your faith?

MEDITATION

Thank you that You are in control even when I'm spiraling out of control. Thank you for Your perfect goodness and compassion that accompany Your sovereignty. Help me cling to You in faith, in all circumstances, no matter what.

Session 4

Naomi's Return

• A Bitter Taste In Her Mouth Called God

So far in this study we've watched three widows, without financial or relational support, trying to keep down the vile circumstances that God has allowed them to swallow. Naomi lost both of her sons and her husband in quick succession. Her grimace grows with every distasteful bite that she is forced to swallow again and again. Eventually, she stands up and barks out loud that this is *not* okay! Compared to other people—not fair. Compared to what is good—not right. And there sits God, seemingly silent, watching her tearfully choke down the sharp permanency of sorrow, bite after bitter bite. It's the time in your life where you question the goodness of God, and for some, the reality of His existence. This opening act takes our breath away in the magnitude of its calamity and we're left stranded without a realistic solution. Today we will investigate how Naomi's bitterness repeatedly shows itself, and consider how her reactions may parallel our own.

Circle Bethlehem and Moab on the map below.

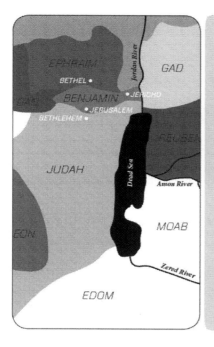

Ruth and Naomi's journey likely left them dirty and exhausted from a seven-to-ten-day trek that spanned thirty miles and included the crossing of the Jordan river with a 2,000 foot slope to climb. They were utterly vulnerable as women travelling alone in the violent days of judges. No lamplights, paved roads, or Starbucks. No city buses, well-colored maps, or rest stops. The treacherous terrain must have mirrored Naomi's heart.

EVIDENCE OF NAOMI'S BITTERNESS

For something to be *bitter*, it means that the flavor of something is not sweet. From an emotional perspective, it carries the connotation of feeling angry, hurt, or resentful because of unfair treatment.[6] There are four key ways that the story displays how Naomi's inward bitterness creeps outward in her behavior.

1) Naomi Tells Her Daughters-In-Law To Turn Back

Read Ruth 1:6–18. Repeating words/phrases often showcases important themes. In the four verses below, circle each use of return, turn back/gone back.

> *"But Naomi said to her two daughters-in-law, "Go, return each of you to her mother's house. May the Lord deal kindly with you, as you have dealt with the dead and with me (1:8)*

> *But Naomi said, "Turn back, my daughters; why will you go with me? Have I yet sons in my womb that they may become your husbands? (1:11)*

> *Turn back, my daughters; go your way, for I am too old to have a husband. If I should say I have hope, even if I should have a husband this night and should bear sons (1:12) ... And she said, "See, your sister-in-law [Orpah] has gone back to her people and to her gods ..." (1:15)*

Take a look again at verse 15 (above). Underline the two things Orpah was returning to.

Naomi is:
1. an Israeli believer who told her daughters-in-law about the true God.
2. a woman who'd won the deep affection and loyalty of Ruth and Orpah.
3. a woman who was faithfully returning to the promised land even in crisis.

Naomi knew God personally and that the Moabites were enemies of God and Israel. Why might Naomi have insisted that they return to Moabite gods? (vss 13, 20)

2) Naomi Openly Changes Her Name to 'Bitter'

Read verses 19–22. To stir means commotion; to excite interest or controversy. How much of the town was "stirred" at her arrival?

Naomi left Bethlehem in famine of food and returned to Bethlehem with famine in her soul. (1:21) She was convinced that God had cursed her personally, and that those associated with her would swallow the same gall. Perhaps she thought that Moabite gods could not give worse affliction than what Israel's God had allowed.

Earlier in this study, we unlocked the importance of meanings, and the name *Naomi* is no exception. While Naomi means *pleasant*, Mara means *unpleasant*[7] or *bitter*.[8] It is important to point out that in Jewish culture, a name defamed was a humongous deal—a public shaming, of sorts. The voluntary admission of Naomi regarding her play-on-words name change, showcases her feelings of destitution and hopelessness. It is raw, open humiliation. She is utterly emptied.[9]

Who does Naomi hold responsible for her bitterness (vs 20)?

Naming Him here is no accident. God sits center stage in her mind, accused as the ultimate cause of her embittered end. Using this name for God was a common Jewish reference that acknowledges His great provision and power.[10] It is also interesting to note that the name of her deceased husband means *My God is king*, referring to God's sovereign rule and authority.[11]

Oh, the biting irony. Although never once denying His sovereignty, Naomi blamed God because in His sovereignty He had allowed her devastation. He was a bully, and she was letting it be known that she was bitter about it. I can feel the tension in her voice as she describes the bitterness to her family and old friends … her *exceeding* bitterness, to be precise.

3) Naomi's Hope For Rest Is Not Placed In God

Name the family members who Naomi directs Ruth and Orpah to for hope and rest. _____ **(vs 8)** _____ **(vss 9, 12)**
_____ **(vs 15)**

How would returning to the person in verse 8 be persuasive for Orpah?

The word *rest* or *menukhah*, that is used by Naomi in verse 9 carries the meaning of *peace* and *happiness*.[12] It is wise for Naomi to recognize that the God-instituted design of marriage and family brings about care, protection, and stability.

Yet, how does her focus also reflect a bitter spirit against God?

4) Naomi's Sarcasm

It seemed to Naomi that God, nor His established system of law for protecting widows, were viable providers of comfort for her.

Now oriented to Levirate-Marriage, what is Naomi's sarcastic point to her daughters-in-law in 1:12–13? Is it a convincing one?

Look back at verses 1–15, and list some key characteristics of Naomi below. Underline those characteristics that you can identify with in your own life.

Did You Know?

LEVIRATE-MARRIAGE Ruth 1:11–13 describes a law established by God as an Old Testament, Jewish custom. (Deut 25:5–10) Its purpose was to protect widows, and ensure that all family lines were valued and propagated. If a Jewish husband died leaving no offspring, the closest male relative of the deceased was to marry the surviving widow, who would bear children in the name of the deceased. Assets of the deceased (i.e. land), were not absorbed into the second husband's estate, but given to the widow's offspring to redeem a broken family line.

KINSMAN-REDEEMER The family member who agreed to Levirate Marriage with the destitute widow was called the Kinsman-Redeemer. As kin, he purchased the widow and paid off any debts associated with her. If the closest kin declined, then the next closest relative was offered the job. The role of Kinsman-Redeemer had significant sacrifices associated with it, making it a great burden and a great privilege.

Personal Reflection

What name would you (or others) give you during times of stress? (Hesitant. Angry. Insecure. Unfaithful. Strong. Determined. Etc.)

"Many workers have gone out with high courage and fine impulses, but with no intimate fellowship with Jesus Christ, and before long they are crushed. They do not know what to do with the burden, it produces weariness, and people say— 'What an embittered end to such a beginning!'...but if we roll back on God that which He has put upon us, He takes away the sense of responsibility by bringing in the realization of Himself." (Oswald Chambers)[13]

Group Discussion

How can we encourage one another to "roll back on God that which He has put on us," especially in times where the tragedy exceeds our own experience?

MEDITATION

Guide our hearts to see You in dark, confusing, and bitter circumstances. Help us discipline our thoughts and attitudes toward wisdom and gratitude.

Session 5

What's in a Name?

When my daughter was two, we bought fish. She carefully observed them in our aquarium. "Mommy! Look at that one with the bright orange and white stripes!"

"Yes, I see that. What are you going to name it sweetie?"

She didn't even hesitate. "Black-y."

I love that girl.

The name my daughter chose was hilarious because it did not match the object. Normally however, when we name, we describe. Names give information and meaning to the things that we label—individuals, families, and nations. We take more liberty with names nowadays, often creating them ourselves based on how they sound—pretty, masculine, or somewhere in the middle. But back in the *days of the judges*, the significance of the meaning associated with names was paramount. Often, biblical names reflected the nature and historical setting of the person or place identified. Today, we are going to take a look at some key names that heavily describe our storyline.

NAMES OF LOCATIONS

Let's examine the origins of the two nations within Ruth. Fill in the blanks.

God's people living in Bethlehem were founded by a man named **Judah.** (1:1) Let's take a look at Judah's life:

- Judah convinced his brothers to sell Joseph to the Ishmaelites. (Gen 37:27)
- Refused to protect and care for Tamar, his dead son's widow as the law said. (Gen 38:11)
- Slept with a woman who was a _____. (Gen 38:15–19)
- Condemned a prostitute publicly for her sexual indiscretion until he was publicly called out as the man who impregnated her, at which time he backed off. (Gen 38:24–26)

The **Moabites** were arch enemies of God's people and founded by a man named Lot. (Gen 19:37) Let's take a look at Lot's life:

- Settled next to the Sodomites—wicked sinners against God. (Gen 13:10–13)

- Offered his two daughters to be raped by sexual predators. (Gen 19:4–8)

- Moabites originated from Lot being tricked into having sex with _____ while drunk. (Gen 19:30–38)

Wow. Both the Moabites *and* God's people showcase some serious family disrepute! God's people, called and named as His own, were founded by great big failures, just like the Moabites, who were sinners just like us.

Personal Reflection

It's not ungodly to delight in your heritage or good behavior—it's our sense of superiority over others that is sinful. Is there an area of your life or family identity that you can acknowledge an unholy sense of superiority?

NAMES OF PEOPLE

Take a look at the names of our secondary characters below and consider how each of their names reflected their future circumstances.

Mahlon (Mah'lon) . . . . . Great infirmity. Sickly.[14]

Chilion (Kil-e-on) . . . . . Pining. Wasting away.[15]

Orpah (Awr-puh) . . . . . Hardened. Double minded.[16]

In Session 4, Naomi faithfully returned home to the promised land, but she was bitter at God who seemed set against her and insistent that Orpah and Ruth return to Moab. Now we will shift gears and focus on Orpah's response to the calamity. Orpah had actually left Moab and was travelling to Bethlehem with Naomi when her decisiveness wavered and she took the easy-road back home. (vs 8–13)

Read 1:8–13. List the arguments that persuaded Orpah to shirk her resolve.

Orpah's decision is made. She returned to the brighter prospect of living the Moabite dream. Perhaps she could start fresh with a new husband, and secure a white picket fence, two-and-a-half healthy kids, a dog, and a future. But her choice came with the price tag of renouncing all previously declared loyalties to Naomi and Almighty God.

Read Matthew 13:3–9, 18–23. What parallel can you make to Orpah's choice?

"If my heart remains unsoftened and unfertilized by grace, the good seed may germinate for a season, but it must ultimately wither for it cannot flourish on a rocky, unbroken, unsanctified heart." (Charles H. Spurgeon)[17]

When you immerse a soft sponge into water and lift it out again, the water pours back into the basin as you tighten your fist. In life, we will all suffer through various trials that are appointed to our lives. The degree to which Christ pours out of our lives during the squeeze of suffering can reflect the degree to which we have immersed ourselves in His presence during times of peace.

THE DEGREE TO WHICH CHRIST POURS OUT OF YOUR LIFE WHILE SUFFERING IS OFTEN A REFLECTION OF THE DEGREE TO WHICH WE HAVE IMMERSED OURSELVES IN HIS PRESENCE DURING TIMES OF PEACE.

"And whoever does not take his cross and follow me is not worthy of me. Whoever finds his life will lose it, and whoever loses his life for my sake will find it. Whoever receives you receives me, and whoever receives me receives him who sent me." (Matt 10:38–40)

"Examine yourselves, to see whether you are in the faith. Test yourselves. Or do you not realize this about yourselves, that Jesus Christ is in you?—unless indeed you fail to meet the test!" (2 Cor 13:5)

Personal Reflection

Do you need to surrender anything in a fresh way to God's control?

MEDITATION

Help our hearts and minds acknowledge You in all circumstances, despite the brokenness and odds that are stacked against us. You are our true hope, protector, comfort, and help in trouble. You are all we need.

Session 6

Ruth's Arrival

• Submission Triumphs

One summer my son had an accident which resulted in partial amputations of three fingers. My heart ached as I walked to his bedside after surgery.

He slowly opened his eyes. "Mommy, do I have full fingers?"

"No, honey, you have stubs." My voice quieted as I fought back tears that begged to push themselves out. "They did their very best, but they couldn't reattach any of them."

His simple response entered the room with a soft and submissive whisper, "Okay."

He's since voiced phrases like, "I'm sad, but I know that this was God's plan for me, so I'm dealing with it."

We grieved. We grieved for the pain he endured, for the memories that linger, for the function that had been permanently altered. As parents, there's nothing worse than seeing your child suffer in any way, and my heart aches for those who endure much worse. The only way we can truly process the pain is to run to Jesus whose presence will fill us with peace and enable us to stand when we collapse. If our aim is happiness, then we've lost. But if our aim is to experience Jesus more closely and display Him more clearly to the world, then we've won. Jesus empowers us to triumph over bitterness in the face of all kinds of heartache.

Today's session explores how Ruth's heart uttered a song of victory amid choking tragedy and shattered dreams. We saw in Ruth 1, how the author penned the word *return* as a predominant, repeating feature in verses 6–22. Specifically, Ruth and Naomi are returning to the promised land that God had originally provided for His people. (Joshua 1:1–6)

SURRENDER

Read Ruth 1:14. Unlike Orpah, what was Ruth's response?

In the original Hebrew, the word *clung* does not mean that Ruth grabbed onto Naomi's body physically. It is the same word used in Genesis 2:24, speaking of a man leaving his father and mother in order to *cling* to his wife. It is a strong word suggesting unity and commitment. Ruth's clinging to Naomi was a demonstration of her unshakeable loyalty and foreshadowed a level of greater self-abandonment to come. While I have compassion for Naomi and Orpah's aching situation, I am profoundly inspired by Ruth's dramatic expression of devotion. It is one of those life-altering choices that flips the rest of your life upside-down.

Fill in the blanks from verses 16 and 17:
    "Your people shall be my people, and _____   _____
    _____   _____."
    "Where you die I will die, and there will I be buried. May the
    _____ do so to me and more also if anything but death parts
    me from you."

This use of LORD refers to the covenant name of Israel's God, and is the same name that God used to describe Himself to Moses at the burning bush—*I am who I am*. Notice that Ruth switches from calling Him *your God*, to claiming him as *her* LORD. This demonstrates more than a sold-out devotion to Naomi, but rather a complete, permanent, committed submission to the God of Israel. In short, she is converting![18] And to make her commitment clear, she calls down curses from her new LORD upon her if she recants. Her future behavior demonstrates that her words were not empty but matched the seriousness of her conversion. This fierce determination silences Naomi abruptly and absolutely.

Dialogue is another predominant, literary feature in Ruth. In Chapter 1, Naomi has more lines than Ruth, but Ruth's are much more show-stopping. Ruth's profound response to Naomi's pressure to *turn back* in verses 16–17 is one of the most well-known and beloved passages in all of Scripture. Ruth replies with a series of five phrases that poetically rise to a climactic finish.

Note the lyrical repetition and rhythm that characterize Ruth's response.

> *"Where you go I will go*
> *Where you lodge I will lodge*
> *Your people shall be my people*
> *And your God my God*
> *Where you die, I will die*
> *And there I will be buried."*

Naomi encouraged Ruth to place her hope in *people*—her mother (vs 8), and a potential new husband. (vss 9, 12) She further insisted that Ruth follow the example of her sister-in-law (vs 15) by returning to Moab in order to recreate a viable life for herself. Naomi's focus was to help Ruth look out for her own self-interests, and put her trust in *others*.

Look at Ruth's response above. How many times are the words *you* or *your* used by Ruth in verses 16–18? _____

Ruth's hope is not placed in herself. Instead, she focuses on surrendering to God and sacrificially serves Naomi as an outpouring of that decision. Notice the increasing intensity of commitment from one phrase to the next:

> I will GO → I will LODGE in a foreign place → I will INTEGRATE into a new group of people → I will SUBMIT to your God → I will DIE trying.

Ruth willingly chose to suffer alongside God's people in famine and carry on in spite of the stigma attached to her Moabite heritage. There is no cerebral bowing to doctrine without the simultaneous bowing of her life to His people and agenda. (James 2:14–26)

Why do some people bow to doctrine but fail to submit their lives to His authority? (2 Tim 3:1–9)

Ruth is grieving the loss of three key men who brought her protection, stability, and the promise of a future. She is also without a job, her family, and the familiar comforts of home. Within the eye of an emotional and circumstantial tornado, she chooses God and simultaneously sacrifices her life to the service of her mother-in-law.

Her last morsel of control is spent sacrificing for another, rather than salvaging what little control she has left for herself. She accepts more crisis–residence within a foreign land and culture, unknown financial and relational security, and the permanent burden of caring for her aging mother-in-law.

She's a role model that seems too lofty for us to emulate because we know we'll fall short—and that is the point. The only way that Ruth had the ability to respond with this kind of sacrificial love and wisdom was because she had been touched by the awesome grace of God who sought and saved her. God powerfully enabled her to understand that if He was *for* her, then no one and nothing could stand against her. (Rom 8:31) Fully counting the cost, she knew that she had not given her life to Israelite doctrine, but to a personal God who now owned her life as LORD. God was enough, and was trustworthy. Ruth responded to being buried under tragedy without bitterness because her life was now wrapped up in the One who'd lifted her buried heart to spiritual freedom.

Read Ruth 2. Look at the list of verses below and briefly summarize the aspects of Ruth's character revealed in each passage.

1:8

1:10

1:14

1:16–18

2:2-3a

2:7

2:17

2:18a

2:23

FOREIGNERS LIKE US

Today we are very accustomed to Christians representing many nations. Yet in Old Testament times, God's people were commanded by God to form a distinct group, separated geographically and culturally from other nations. A Moabite woman converting and integrating into Israelite society must have shaken the bedrock of many Jews' understanding of God. Moabites were excluded from the nation of Israel (Deut 23:3), but Ruth's acceptance is evidence of God's extension of grace to the non-Jews (Gentiles) and to us! (Acts 10:9–48; Eph 2:11–22) Do you see the connection between our lives and this story? We—as Gentiles—are represented in this play by the Moabites! Not exactly the part you'd choose to audition for, but our lives parallel theirs on several levels. We were foreigners to holiness, *great sinners* against God, objects of His wrath, and sentenced eternally. But then we were accepted and grafted into His heavenly kingdom, to be coheirs with Christ forever. (Eph 2:1–7, Rom 8:16-17)

Personal Reflection

How does reflection on your *Moabite* status impact your response to God?

MEDITATION

You not only saved us from the penalty of our sin, but called us friends and made us coheirs to Your kingdom. Thank You for lavishing Your grace and love upon us.

Session 7

3 Widows, 3 Responses, 1 You

Despite initially good intentions, Orpah's resolve to stay with Naomi collapsed and she returned to worshipping other gods. Naomi willingly returned to God and His people, but with a bitter and unyielding heart. Ruth fully surrendered to God without bitterness, and remained faithful to both God and His people until the end of the story. In Colossians 3:2 we read, "*Set your mind on things that are above, not on things that are on the earth.*" In Ruth 1, each woman's response to crisis directly correlated to where she focused her mind.

In the spaces below, describe the *things above* or *things on earth* that each woman focused on. Briefly comment how this focus influenced their outcome.

Orpah *(Hardened. Double minded.)*[19]

Naomi *(Agreeable. Pleasantness of Jehovah.)*[20]

Ruth *(Supreme virtuous woman. Satisfied.)*[21, 22]

WE ARE NOT MEANT TO ESCAPE THE DARKNESS BECAUSE OUR CHIEF AIM IS NOT EARTHLY HAPPINESS. WE ARE MEANT TO SUBMIT TO CHRIST IN THE MIDST OF THE DARKNESS, SO THAT OUR LIVES BECOME CHANNELS OF LIGHT IN DARK PLACES.

The characters we've studied are relatable. We can identify with the exhausted bitterness of Naomi, the logical hesitancy of Orpah, and are inspired by Ruth's faithful resolve to submit to the LORD in spite of oppressing circumstances. What we need to discover is how Ruth aligned her mind and heart rightly before God, and how we can learn from her example. We are not meant to escape the darkness because our chief aim is not earthly happiness. We are meant to submit to Christ in the midst of the darkness, so that our lives become channels of light in dark places. What circumstances are positioned against you? What attitudes paralyze you?

Difficulties are real, overwhelming, and personal. We cannot climb out of the darkness on our own ability—we need to cling to God who hovers in the dark with us. Like Ruth, we need to see beyond present, bitter setbacks that choke our relationship with Christ, and submit to God's sovereign plan over our lives individually, as families, and as a nation. Because we can trust His mercy and compassion in our daily lives, we are free—free to forfeit any attitude, possession, or sense of entitlement that we hold dear. We must take Christ's life in exchange for ours even though we may become poor and despised and feel like all is lost. Belonging to Christ is permanently tethered to His mastery over our goals. We will either head toward the land of promise with God for us, or we will turn back to the land of compromise with God against us.

"When you go through a trial, the sovereignty of God is the pillow upon which you lay your head."
(Charles Spurgeon)[23]

Read the verses below.

"The heart of man plans his way, but the Lord establishes his steps." (Prov 16:9)

"As for you, you meant evil against me, but God meant it for good, to bring it about that many people should be kept alive, as they are today." (Gen 50:20)

"... who brings princes to nothing, and makes the rulers of the earth as emptiness." (Is 40:23)

"... and said, "O Lord, God of our fathers, are you not God in heaven? You rule over all the kingdoms of the nations. In your hand are power and might, so that none is able to withstand you." (2 Ch 20:6)

Personal Reflection

How does God's sovereignty inform your current circumstances?

Group Discussion

What practices or people might help you stay focused on *things above*?

MEDITATION

You are the Almighty Ruler yet an intimate companion. Help us to fully surrender our circumstances to You, so that we can rest our weary souls on the pillow of Your sovereignty.

Session 8

Crushed, But Not Destroyed

When I was little I loved wave pools. The unpredictable push and pull of the strong waves tossed me back and forth creating a thrilling experience. There was safety in knowing that a lifeguard supervised the currents and controlled its cessation when trouble arose for swimmers. As an adult my opinion about wave pools has changed—the lack of control over my body is quite disconcerting, and the length of time it takes to extract my haggard self from its rocking grip feels more exhausting than delightful.

By the end of Chapter 1, Naomi is unimpressed with the wave pool of emotion that is tossing her back and forth. She is drowning from the undertow of exhaustion and sorrow. Left empty and exceedingly bitter, it is uncertain whether any good will rise in her life again. Today's session showcases a wave pool of emotions for our characters. Just when they are drowning under the pull of one wave, a current of hope lifts them up to breathe oxygen and then they're tossed them back into the water again. The waves of promise that appear in Chapter 2, crash against the ongoing waves of sorrow from Chapter 1. Later, we will meet the Lifeguard who oversees the currents and ensures our safe passage through the rocky ride.

Did You Know?

GLEANING Ruth based her words in 2:2, on a protective law that God had established to allow the poor to freely pick up any left-over grain that paid workers left behind in the harvest fields (Lev 19:9, 23:22; Deut 24:21). God demanded by law that the poor be treated with mercy. The corners of fields were also not to be reaped (Lev 19:9-10, 23:22; Deut 24:19-21). Similar laws were given regarding vineyards and olive yards. Basing her words on this law, Ruth the Moabitess said to her mother-in-law Naomi: *"Let me go to the field and glean among the ears of grain after him in whose sight I find favor."* (Ruth 2:2) Essentially, to glean was to beg.

A dialogue between Ruth and Boaz is predominant in the second chapter of Ruth. We also see Ruth's hard and eager work ethic. Ruth is working overtime in a manual labor job, swimming in thick waves of grief, and serving her aging mother-in-law who can't pull her weight. Yet somehow, she continues to evade bitterness. Theatrical productions typically have set-hands who replace backdrops between scenes when appropriate. Chapter 1 opened with a despairing backdrop of death and darkness, but now the curtain closes and the set-hands race to replace the gloomy 'time of the judges' with the hopeful 'time of the barley-harvest'. The barley-harvest refers to a happy time of gathering, feasting, and blessing. It is against the backdrop of this new barley-harvest that Boaz—our new character and hero, is introduced. In a story where names speak volumes, we cannot overlook the meaning of Boaz: "In Him (The LORD) is strength."[24]

In 2:3 we read that Ruth happened to glean in Boaz's field. The word *happened* implies chance, but it was the guidance of our sovereign God who held and directed her.

Did You Know?

BARLEY-HARVEST Barley was one of the two staple grain crops in biblical times (wheat was the other). The barley-harvest corresponded to the end of our March, and was a season when the community praised God for His provision and goodness. In April, the barley crop ripened and was ready for harvest. The wheat harvest followed approximately 2 weeks later.

Consider the concept of Levirate Marriage that was introduced in Session 4. Why does hope ignite when we learn that Boaz is a *relative of her* (Naomi) *husbands*, of *the clan of Elimelech?* (vs 2:1)

The author masterfully pens cumulating waves of hope, just as clearly as he introduced the cumulating waves of despair in Chapter 1. Summarize the *waves* in the spaces below.

Waves of Despair

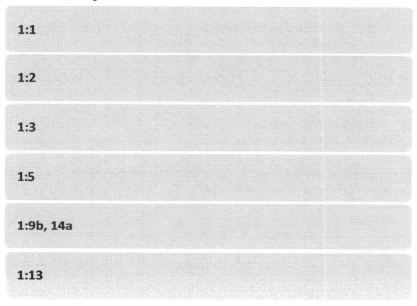

1:1

1:2

1:3

1:5

1:9b, 14a

1:13

Waves of Hope

1:6

1:17

1:22

2:1

2:3

We have begun to see God stir circumstantial waters to the favor of Ruth and Naomi. You see, God is sovereignly in control of our despair *and* our blessings. When He allows calamity, He also experiences it with us, sustains us within it, and will one day deliver us completely from it.

> *"We are afflicted in every way, but not crushed; perplexed, but not driven to despair; persecuted, but not forsaken; struck down, but not destroyed; always carrying in the body the death of Jesus, so that the life of Jesus may also be manifested in our bodies." (2 Cor 4:8–10)*

Personal Reflection

How can we remain encouraged and faithful when waves of despair overwhelm our perspective?

Group Discussion

Have you ever felt knocked over by life circumstances and yet simultaneously been granted the strength and grace to move forward? Discuss.

MEDITATION

Help us learn the discipline of gratitude so that we may trust You more, by always remembering who You are and what You have done for us.

Session 9

Boaz

- Part I

We opened this study by comparing the process of Bible study with the completion of a puzzle. Today the story reaches a climax because Boaz, the main image of the puzzle, finally comes into place!

Back to our story. So far, we have set the stage with backgrounds, characters, and plot line. Ruth and Naomi have suffered unexpected life trauma, but promises of hope have now been ushered in with the barley-harvest, the opportunity to glean in Boaz's field, and with the discovery of Boaz's family connection to Ruth. Boaz enters the stage as a kind, godly, and wise businessman—impressive qualities given the spiritually depraved time period that he lived within. Through Boaz's character we witness how God can transform everyday people into extraordinary manifestations of His power and beauty.

On the right, describe what each set of verses reveals about Boaz's character. (Hint: Be specific. In 2:1, there are four traits—one is simply that he is a man.)

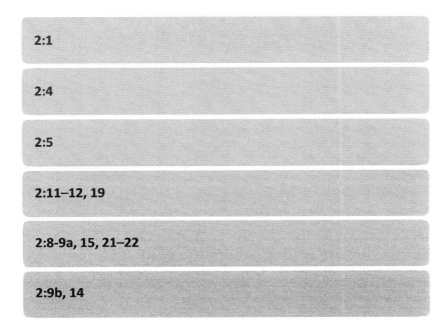

2:1

2:4

2:5

2:11–12, 19

2:8-9a, 15, 21–22

2:9b, 14

CAN'T WASH OFF MOABITE

Fill in the blanks.

*"Yes Boaz, she is the young _____ _____
(2:6) woman, who came back with Naomi from the country of
_____." (2:6) Ruth bows to the ground in verse 10,
exclaiming, "Why have I found favor ... since I am a
_____." (2:10)*

Fill in the rest of the sentence. In verse 13 she again echoes the
unprecedented kindness of Boaz even *"though I am
_____."* (2:13)

Ruth is overwhelmed by Boaz's kindness and generosity. These were
the days when the judges ruled in Israel, and she couldn't wash off
Moabite.

THE WINGS OF GOD

Ruth left her family, friends, native land, and gods, to live among
foreigners and give her life to God. (2:11) Because this came at a
great personal cost, Boaz esteems her highly and blesses her for
having come under the refuge of God's wings. (vs 12)

Describe what we learn about wings in the following verses:

*"You yourselves have seen what I did to the Egyptians, and
how I bore you on eagles' wings and brought you to myself."
(Ex 19:4)*

*"Keep me as the apple of your eye; hide me in the shadow of
your wings." (Ps 17:8)*

*"How precious is your steadfast love, O God! The children of
mankind take refuge in the shadow of your wings."
(Ps 36:7)*

*"Be merciful to me, O God, be merciful to me, for in you my
soul takes refuge; in the shadow of your wings I will take
refuge, till the storms of destruction pass by." (Ps 57:1)*

It is easy to applaud Ruth's toil and drive, and be inspired to try harder and work better. Yet, when Naomi sees the huge load of barley that Ruth gleaned (Ruth 2:17–20), notice that Naomi never once applauds Ruth's hard work ethic. Ruth rose to work early in the morning (2:7), only took short breaks (2:7), and worked well into the evening. (2:17) Despite Ruth's hard work, it is blatantly obvious that the amount she had reaped was because someone had been helping her, moving circumstances beyond Ruth's knowledge and involvement. Further, in verse 12, we see Boaz clarify that Ruth's admirable work ethic is secondary to her taking refuge under the wings of God. Her strength is attributable to the power she finds in Him, not by trusting in her own might. Ruth's humble servanthood confirms her understanding of the grace and favor that she received. We must work diligently and invest our gifts faithfully, yet always give full praise to God who graciously bestows any blessings we receive.

Personal Reflection

Is there pride you need to confess associated with your abilities or gifts?

Group Discussion

Does God's goodness toward us despite the fact that we are sinners, compel us to greater godliness or lukewarm living? (Rom 6 may help you answer.)

MEDITATION

Thank You for covering us with Your wings of forgiveness, protection, and grace now and always. Help us to give You praise for Your goodness when You work through us.

Session 10

Boaz

• Part 2

Let's jump right into finishing our discussion about Boaz. In Ruth 2:20, Naomi tells Ruth that Boaz is *one of our redeemers*. Remember from Session 1 that Jewish law allowed a close family member to buy back land that was sold by a poverty-stricken relative. Elimelech may have sold his family's land out of desperation prior to leaving for Moab. The Redeemer who buys back the land—and people associated with it—propagates the physical and financial line of the deceased. It is a costly privilege and burden.[25]

In verses 19 and 20, how and why do we see Naomi's attitude shifting?

Right in the middle of the despair steps Boaz—noticing, caring, identifying, saving, transforming. Yet the point of Ruth is that we will *never* be like Boaz. No matter how hard we resolve, nor how gifted we think we are, at the end of the day, we are the Moabites, and we fall desperately short of being holy like God. (Rom 3:23) We can't wipe off Moabite no matter how hard we scrub. Ruth and Naomi do not need a pat on the back, nor a word of encouragement, they need redemption. Boaz is the hero of this story because he is the only one with the authority to give Ruth access to his harvest field, approve her invitation to feast with him, and enjoy his intimate company.

We now see *our* Rescuer face-to-face in Boaz—the Christ-figure for Ruth, Naomi, you, and me. Christ stepped into human skin to redeem and transform the darkness within and around us—eternal death, our dark circumstances, and the darkness lurking within our souls. He is *our* kinsman-redeemer because He is the only One with adequate resources of authority, ability, and mercy to accept the obligation to redeem us Moabites, despite the sacrificial cost to Himself. (Gal 4:1–7) He married us when we were stuck in the dying line of humankind, raised our eternally doomed lives back to life with Him, and now invites us into His presence to feast with Him in intimate fellowship. While we can invest our lives diligently in spiritual work for Him, any blessing we reap is not because of our hard work, but because of Christ's generous favor to work all things together for good, often in realms that we cannot perceive.

The passages below describe the relationship between Boaz and Ruth, and Christ with us. Fill in each box with one of the phrases below that summarizes how our lives parallel Ruth's.

- Cost of Redemption

- Marriage to Christ

- Inheritance in Christ

- Fulfilled Public/Legal Requirements of Redemption

1) BOAZ & RUTH

"So I (Boaz) thought I would tell you of it and say, 'Buy it in the presence of those sitting here and in the presence of the elders of my people.' If you will redeem it, redeem it. But if you will not, tell me, that I may know, for there is no one besides you to redeem it, and I come after you." … Then the redeemer said, "I cannot redeem it for myself, lest I impair my own inheritance. Take my right of redemption yourself, for I cannot redeem it." (Ruth 4:4a,6)

CHRIST & US

"… remember that you were at that time separated from Christ, alienated from the commonwealth of Israel and strangers to the covenants of promise, having no hope and without God in the world. But now in Christ Jesus you who once were far off have been brought near by the blood of Christ. For he himself is our peace, who has made us both one and has broken down in his flesh the dividing wall of hostility." (Eph 2:12–14)

2) BOAZ & RUTH

"Now this was the custom in former times in Israel concerning redeeming and exchanging: to confirm a transaction, the one drew off his sandal and gave it to the other, and this was the manner of attesting in Israel. So when the redeemer said to Boaz, "Buy it for yourself," he drew off his sandal. Then Boaz said to the elders and all the people, "You are witnesses this day that I have bought from the hand of Naomi all that belonged to Elimelech and all that belonged to Chilion and to Mahlon." (Ruth 4: 7–9)

CHRIST & US

"After this, Jesus, knowing that all was now finished, said (to fulfill the Scripture), "I thirst." A jar full of sour wine stood there, so they put a sponge full of the sour wine on a hyssop branch and held it to his mouth. When Jesus had received the sour wine, he said, "It is finished," and he bowed his head and gave up his spirit." (John 19:28–30)

3) BOAZ & RUTH

*"So Boaz took Ruth, and she became his wife."
(Ruth 4:13a)*

CHRIST & US

"Husbands, love your wives, as Christ loved the church and gave himself up for her, that he might sanctify her, having cleansed her by the washing of water with the word, so that he might present the church to himself in splendor, without spot or wrinkle or any such thing, that she might be holy and without blemish." (Eph 5:25–27)

"For as a young man marries a young woman, so shall your sons marry you, and as the bridegroom rejoices over the bride, so shall your God rejoice over you." (Is 62:5)

4) BOAZ & RUTH

"And he went in to her, and the Lord gave her conception, and she bore a son. Then the women said to Naomi, "Blessed be the Lord, who has not left you this day without a redeemer, and may his name be renowned in Israel!... They named him Obed. He was the father of Jesse, the father of David." (Ruth 13a,14,17b)

CHRIST & US

"Therefore he is the mediator of a new covenant, so that those who are called may receive the promised eternal inheritance, since a death has occurred that redeems them from the transgressions committed under the first covenant." (Heb 9:15)

In the love story of Ruth, we experience Christ's portrayal of Himself to us—His pursuing, committed, protective love. As our understanding of Him grows, our worship will follow. How exciting that the Lord sought to teach us about Himself, through a story that ignites our senses, and takes us on an adventure of tragedy and hope! God sovereignly orchestrated these events in history, in order to give us unbridled permission to glimpse *Him* as the One who woos and wins us over to His love and refuge. He doesn't want our affection for Boaz to transfer into longing for another human being. He wants our affection for Boaz to be fully linked to *Him* as our Bridegroom, the ultimate love of our life. We are betrothed to Him, and coheirs to all that God has. Our groom is committed to faithfully love and cherish us always as His bride.

> *"So I (Boaz) thought I would tell you of it and say, 'Buy it in the presence of those sitting here and in the presence of the elders of my people.' If you will redeem it, redeem it. But if you will not, tell me, that I may know, for there is no one besides you to redeem it, and I come after you ..." Then the redeemer said, "I cannot redeem it for myself, lest I impair my own inheritance. Take my right of redemption yourself, for I cannot redeem it." (Ruth 4:4a,6)*

Look back at the chart about Boaz from Session 9. Put a ✓ beside each of the characteristics that reflect Christ.

Personal Reflection

On the same Session 9 chart, underline those characteristics of Christ that most powerfully impact your circumstances right now.

MEDITATION

Thank You for sending Christ to save us from the darkness within and around us! Thank You for pursuing and committing Yourself to us. Help this knowledge of You to remain deep and fresh in our hearts, regardless of our circumstances.

Session 11

Seeking Rest, Finding Grace

At the start of Chapter 2, the barley-harvest brought in hope and promise. By the end of Chapter 2 Naomi's attitude shifted from bitterness to blessing. We were delighted to see a godly man like Boaz protecting and caring for a Moabite like Ruth, and even more wonderful to grasp Christ's intentional pursuit of us. Now we'll move on to witness an unusual proposal as the climax of our love story.

Read Ruth 3.

Did You Know?

THRESHING FLOOR This was an open air, slightly raised platform that the people of Bethlehem took turns using for threshing and winnowing grain. Threshing the grain was the process of beating the grain out of its stocks at the close of the day, with a stick or stones.

WINNOWING This was the process of tossing the grain in the air and letting the cooler, evening wind blow away the chaff. The grain would then be gathered in heaps to be sold or stored in granaries. The time of threshing and winnowing was a time of big celebration and festivity.

SEEKING REST

Rest—the kind of word that evokes feelings of serenity and restoration. The *aaahhh* moments where *being* trumps *doing*, and we quietly heal. No difficulties, no deadlines, no disappointments. Space and time are ours.

Read the verses below and underline *rest* each time it appears.

> *"Go, return each of you to her mother's house. May the Lord deal kindly with you, as you have dealt with the dead and with me. The Lord grant that you may find rest, each of you in the house of her husband!" (1:8b-9)*

> *"Then Naomi her mother-in-law said to her, "My daughter, should I not seek rest for you, that it may be well with you? (3:1)*

> *"She replied, "Wait, my daughter, until you learn how the matter turns out, for he will not rest but will settle the matter today." (3:18)*

Rest has been Naomi's pre-occupation throughout this story, and now we see her actively engaged in planning for their future. Finding rest in earthly things is not wrong, but must be kept in proper priority to the rest we seek in Christ. Naomi and Ruth's most satisfying rest arrives in Boaz who alone could provide them with the protection, provision, and care that they longed for.

Did You Know?

UNCOVERING BOAZ'S FEET The rationale behind uncovering Boaz's feet is somewhat lost in antiquity, and has sparked much debate among scholars. The dialogue between Ruth and Boaz is a ceremonial act of proposing marriage.

Boaz likely slept on the threshing floor to guard the grain at night from thieves. Some suggest that Ruth's choice to lie by Boaz alone at night was highly brazen, while others determine that this interpretation is completely inconsistent with Ruth's character. (3:11) It is plausible to consider that Naomi would have completely trusted Boaz's behavior to be godly, and that the hidden time of night would have given Boaz the opportunity to reject her proposal without public humiliation. Perhaps the forwardness of Ruth's proposal

is because she knew that Boaz would likely not initiate a proposal when he wasn't the closest redeemer (vs 12), nor her age (vs 10), nor likely in private company with him at any time. Regardless of the details, we know that upon hearing her proposal, Boaz blesses her for kindness, rather than reprimands her for indiscretion. (vs 10)

PROPOSING HOPE

Naomi's strategy was not typical for a proposal, even back then! Remember that the author is always persuading us to release our emotional selves in connection to this story. Consider the torrent of emotions that must have been exploding inside of Ruth—she was a real woman, with a fragile heart, and an uncertain end. But she had learned to surrender to God and submitted to the wisdom of Naomi anyway. So, she scampered to the threshing floor at night where Boaz was sleeping, lay there until he noticed her, and courageously popped the question! Having taken protection under God's wings, Ruth is now asking for protection under the man God provided.

Fill in the blank with the term from 3:9 that Ruth uses to describe herself in relation to Boaz. _____

Read the following verses.

> [Boaz] "The Lord repay you for what you have done, and a full reward be given you by the Lord, the God of Israel, under whose wings you have come to take refuge!" (2:12)

> He [Boaz] said, "Who are you?" And she answered, 'I am Ruth, your servant. Spread your wings over your servant, for you are a redeemer." (3:9)

How are Ruth 2:12 and Ruth 3:9 connected?

The phrase, *corner of your garment* can also be translated *wing*.

Listen to God in Ezekiel about His relationship with His unfaithful people:

> "When I passed by you again and saw you, behold, you were at the age for love, and I spread the corner of my garment over you and covered your nakedness; I made my vow to you and entered into a covenant with you, declares the Lord God, and you became mine." (Ez 16:8)

Here we see yet another glimpse of Christ through Boaz's actions. Ruth submits herself to Boaz's care and protection, and this godly man responds by covering with these things in marriage. For us, as we submit ourselves to God, He covers us with His holiness, and commits to have and hold us until death finally brings us home to His arms.

WORTHY OF HOPE & REST

In 3:11, Boaz states that *"all my fellow townsmen know that you are a worthy woman."* She is not only worthy, but she is well known for her worthy character. So there we have it—the worthy man of 2:1 may now be marrying the *worthy* woman of 3:11! Boaz and Ruth are a match made in heaven.

What does this have to do with us today? Christ is the worthy Bridegroom, and we are His bride. But the problem for us Moabites, is that we are anything but worthy. We have been *declared* worthy, and coheirs with Christ by no effort of our own. Boaz's blessing upon Ruth was because she had sought shelter in God, not pulled herself up by the bootstraps and worked harder. The possibility of our worthiness is explained by one of the most tremendous and fundamental doctrines of Christianity—*Substitution*. Because Christ died on the cross in our place, our punishment was paid. Not only did we not get what we deserved (which reflects His mercy), God lavished extra blessings of His presence and kingdom toward us (which reflects His grace). Now, when God looks at us He sees the perfection of Christ, because when God looked at the cross He saw Christ paying our consequences. (2 Cor 5:21) I am not just declared worthy, I *am* worthy. Christ is worthy of our worship!

Did You Know?

In the Hebrew Bible, the book of Ruth was intentionally placed directly after the book of Proverbs so that readers would naturally move from reading about the *woman of noble character* in Proverbs 31, to reading about the woman who exemplified these characteristics—Ruth herself.

LAVISHING GRACE

In 3:15–18, Boaz lavishes oodles of barley on Ruth to convey his love and intent to marry her, along with communicating to Naomi that she would be cared for as well. (vs 17) The character of Boaz demonstrates how Christ not only sets us free from the penalty of our sin, but went further to lavish us with His abundant riches and position us as heirs to His eternal kingdom.

Ruth could confidently approach Boaz with Naomi's plan because she faithfully clung to God's will regardless of the discomfort or lack of logic.

Did You Know?

Six measures of barley (vs 15) was the rough equivalent of about 60 pounds of grain—a two week supply—which is a huge load for Ruth to carry back home!

Group Discussion

Can you describe a time where you (or someone you know) took an unusual leap of faith that in retrospect the hand of God can be seen more clearly?

MEDITATION

How do we say thank You for Your mercy and Your grace? You're powerful and You're intimate. You're faithful in our faithlessness. Press upon our souls a fuller understanding of who You are.

Session 12

The Cost

We've changed course from the *days of the judges* to the festive season of harvest. Naomi once ached with bitterness and sought isolation, but now is coaching Ruth's love affair with focus and enthusiasm. From the cumulative despair of multiple deaths, to the brightness of a Christ-figure whose rescue and lavish grace rises higher than our imaginations could have carried us. The foreign woman once eternally lost is now permanently grafted into God's kingdom. We just *know* that this story ends well, and our hearts can't wait to have the final scene of romantic happiness unveiled.

Did You Know?

TOWN GATE OF BETHLEHEM This was where civil and personal business matters occurred. When Boaz called the elders together in 4:2 at the town gate, he officiated a public, legal transaction which necessitated witnesses.

Read Ruth 4.

In verse 4, the love wheels fall off entirely. Here is the climax of our love story, the final scene that is supposed to end in hugs and smooches as Boaz legally acquires Ruth and Elimelech's land for himself.

But *Mr. Nearer-Redeemer* says what in Ruth 4:4?

And our hearts sink. This is the second time (3:12 & 4:4) that *Mr. Three's-A-Crowd* shows up and ruins the mojo. Perhaps a tragic end after all? Thankfully the book of Ruth is a succinct little story so we're not left in angst for too long. Boaz is masterful and careful in his explanation to *Mr. Unwelcome* about Ruth's circumstances. He begins with detailing the opportunity to redeem the land which *Mr. Not-Good-Enough* nobly accepts. But he leaves the overwhelming news until the end—the financial and personal burden of raising Ruth's future children and giving them back their rightful land. In short, he can't be the Kinsman-Redeemer because his resources are inadequate to accept the costly burden associated with the purchase— an inadequacy that mirrors our own before God. Our hard work toward holiness gets us the same place we started—falling short of the perfect character of God and locked inside the penalty of our sin.

The sound of the last words from *Mr. Falls-Short's* mouth cues hope, "*Buy it for yourself*." The final tension at the climax of our story has reached its resolution, and it's time for the love birds to set sail into their worthy sunset. It's interesting to note that in a storyline full of names with rich meaning, *Mr. Aren't-You-Gone-Yet?* doesn't get one. This *Almost-Redeemer* comes close to redeeming rightfully, but the burdens associated with the sacrifice choked out the blessings he could have received from counting the cost. No name. No cost. No blessing.

Read the verses below. Describe the *cost* that was refused to be laid down.

- *Matt 19:16–22*

- *Luke 15:25–32 (Hint: focus on the brother's attitude, not the son who squandered his inheritance.)*

These men may have maintained an outward spirituality and sense of control over their circumstances, yet sadness and anger permeated their rebellious hearts.

THE TRANSACTION OF THE COST

The legal transaction of Boaz's acquiring Ruth was finalized in 4:7-10 by Boaz taking off his sandal in front of a town full of witnesses, and verbally declaring it as complete. Personally, I much prefer the modern procedure of signing administrative papers over a sweaty shoe gift between a couple of grown men. However, in Ruth's culture, this shoe-giving process finalized a legal transaction with a memorable, symbolic act.[26] For Boaz to redeem Naomi and Ruth, the law had to be *publicly* satisfied and not bypassed. (Ruth 4:8–10) With shoe in hand, Boaz now had the right to walk on Elimelech's land as his own property.

Similarly, when Christ proclaimed *"It is finished"* (John 19:30), He was declaring that a legal transaction was taking place through a memorable, symbolic act. The demands of God's law (Deut 25) were publicly satisfied with the price of His blood. (1 Pet 1:18–19) Like Ruth, we now have a new identity, position, and status—not as Mrs. Boaz, but as the redeemed bride of Christ Himself. In response, we give Him the right to walk through the center of our lives with His presence, power, and purpose.

THE TRANSFORMATION OF THE COST

I have always enjoyed movie scripts with unexpected twists and turns. There's enjoyment in becoming emotionally connected to the characters and their saga. Is the good guy a villain in disguise? How will the relational mayhem resolve?

In our story, we have identified with the Moabites who were foreigners against God and destined for wrath. By the promised love of Christ, we (along with Ruth), can be grafted by grace into His kingdom. Indeed, it is Christ who shines into our hearts as the hero of love and hope. Still, our story has a plot twist that you may find surprising. While Boaz is the heroic savior of our story, he is *not* the main character of the book. Curious? Let's dig deeper.

Read each verse below and name the primary person of that segment.

1:5	3:1
1:19-22	3:18
2:1	4:3
2:22-23	4:16-17

We journey alongside one primary character throughout the book of Ruth—Naomi! While Boaz is our hero and Christ-figure, it is the story of Naomi's life that begins and finishes the book as a whole and has key presence within each chapter. We resonate with her humanity throughout the journey—her brokenness, bitterness, witness, community, family stress, and more. She is not our hero. She is someone who struggles, someone who desperately needs hope and redemption, someone relatable. Someone like us.

Let's take a quick look at how she has been transformed. Look at the verses below and briefly summarize her attitudes and actions.

- Ruth 2:19-20, 22

- Ruth 3:1-4,16,18

- Ruth 4:16-17

Consider Naomi's spiritual timeline from Tragedy → Bitterness → Hope → Re-engagement → Blessing.

Naomi becomes Obed's nurse (4:16) which some scholars suggest implies a formal adoption.[27] Yet we also know that Naomi was older and may not have been able to assume a primary caregiver role. Regardless of how Naomi practically enacted her role as nurse, this adoption was ultimately to demonstrate that Obed was perpetuating Elimelech's line. Ruth 4:17 says it well, *"A son has been born to Naomi"*. Obed means *'worshipper'*.[28]

SOVEREIGN THROUGH ALL OF OUR COSTS

It is interesting to note that although the book of Ruth is primarily written in dialogue, God Himself does not have any direct lines. Yet God permeates the text anyway! His sovereignty shines out of the characters' language and we've watched how every 'coincidence' was really a part of God's intentional master design. Within the text, the term *LORD* is used 18 times, *God* is used twice, and *Almighty* twice. *Behold* (or happened) occurs three times. (2:3, 2:4, 4:1) Is this not like our lives today? While we may not hear His voice thunder audibly into our ears about every life decision, His presence is with us and He is constantly moving invisible realms for His purposes.

Group Discussion

As Naomi reflects on her tragedy from a Chapter 4 viewpoint, what might she say to her Chapter 1 self that may help her react better?

"Have we come to the place where God can withdraw His blessings and it does not affect our trust in Him? When once we see God at work, we will never bother our heads about things that happen, because we are actually trusting in our Father in Heaven whom the world cannot see."
(Oswald Chambers)[29]

MEDITATION

Thank You for the rest Your sovereignty brings when crisis hits and confusion reigns. Help us to enter into Your rest and increase our intimacy and trust in You.

Session 13

The Story of Me Affects You

Today we place some final pieces into our puzzle and investigate the impact of communal blessing. Throughout the book of Ruth, we see exchanges of blessing between: Boaz and his workers (2:4); Naomi and her daughters-in-law (1:8); Naomi for Boaz (2:19–20); Boaz and Ruth (2:11-13 and 3:9-10); and the Israelite community with Boaz and Ruth. (4:11,14,17) So often, jealousy, gossip, and ungodly efforts to control seem to overpower our energy toward unity. In today's session, we observe a community overcome with genuine joy at God's sovereign provision and blessing in someone *else's* life.

THE BLESSING OF COMMUNITY

"All of the people who were at the gate and the elders" (4:11–12) witnessed this transaction and responded in a united, prayerful blessing.

Look up these verses and describe how each blessing was fulfilled later.

- 1:9

- 2:4

- 2:12

- How is 4:11 fulfilled in 4:13–17?

Look at each blessing for Boaz and Ruth on the left and draw a line to its corresponding meaning on the right.

"May the LORD make the woman, who is coming into your house, like Rachel and Leah, who together built up the house of Israel ..." (4:11a)

Ephrathah and Bethlehem are used interchangeably in Scripture. (Gen 48:7; Micah 5:2) The use of *worthily* here is the same word for *valor, worth, or ability*. It suggests a prayer for Boaz and Ruth to become famous. The result? Their story was sealed in the scriptural canon forever.[30]

The mentioning of Rachel and Leah has significance because Rachel, like Ruth, was barren for many years before she bore children. Rachel and Leah were also significant matriarchs of the 12 tribes of Israel. They were praying that Obed's line would produce significant spiritual offspring that would bless many nations.[31] The result? Eventually, all the nations of the world would be blessed through Christ.

"May you act worthily in Ephrathah and be renowned in Bethlehem ..." (4:11b)

"May your house be like the house of Perez, whom Tamar bore to Judah, because of the offspring that the LORD will give you by this young woman." (4:12)

Perez was the son of a once broken family line just like Obed (Tamar's husband died and her brother-in-law Judah was Perez' dad). Perez was an ancestor of Boaz—the wealthy Christ-figure of this story. (Matt 1:1–16)[32] They prayed that Obed's line would also lead to someone great. The result? Christ Himself came out of this line.

It is interesting to consider how many of the blessings we enjoy today are attributable to the faithful prayers of the community that preceded us. Take time this week to ask God to bless your family's line in seen and unseen ways, to the glory of His name. How exciting it will be to one day discover how those prayers were brought to fruition.

God wove the need for community into the fabric of every heart. Friends. Spouses. Children. Family. Beautiful people, designed by God, and appointed to our lives. Relationships are sacred in their importance. God Himself reflects community being the Father, the Son, and the Holy Spirit. Community is not only in His heart, but central to the very nature of who He is. It makes sense that God works out His purposes within a communal context. He compels people's hearts to pray, and then fulfills His purposes through His people.

Group Discussion

Discuss how you have seen your Christian community speak blessings over one another, and whether that needs to be more of a priority.

THE EFFORT OF COMMUNITY

God designed community, yet in the absence of family and spiritual support, Ruth clung to God and sacrificed for the embittered Naomi anyway. Do we enjoy our community in proper priority with our communion with Christ? Practically, do we find more rest in human relationships? Do we really believe that Christ alone can satisfy us when we are at our weakest and our support systems are failing? Are we humble enough to forbear with those who we deem inadequate and fail us repeatedly?

Fill in the blanks with *N* (Naomi) or *R* (Ruth), depending on what accurately completes the sentence. Events date from earliest to latest.

1) _____ points _____ to God when Ruth is a Moabite against God ... ***then*** ...

2) _____ points to God when Naomi is bitter against God. Ruth works sacrificially for Naomi by gleaning diligently in the fields ... ***then*** ...

3) _____ teaches _____ about Jewish laws and customs, guiding her to action to find rest in Boaz ... ***then*** ...

4) Boaz blesses _____ and _____ by being their kinsman-redeemer ... ***then*** ...

5) Boaz and _____ bless _____ with a continued family line.

The book of Ruth is a story about redemption, and it is intriguing to understand that Naomi did not require redemption in the same way as Ruth. Ruth was redeemed from her status as a Moabite by being grafted into Judaism. Naomi required redemption from her bitter attitude. Naomi had known better, and should have done better, yet she was nourished, blessed, and restored anyway through the community God positioned around her. The progression we see between Ruth and Naomi influencing one another back and forth, is nothing short of divine in its forbearance and grace. If one of these five points of influence was removed, this story would be over.

There are times when biblical wisdom dictates that we need to dissociate from certain people for various legitimate reasons such as divisive character (Titus 3:10); lack of repentance (1 Cor 5:11), or being ostracized for choosing Christ. (Matt 10:34-38) Often however, our reasons for disunity are not noble, but sinful in nature. Verses 14–17 showcase another communal glimpse of love and blessing, and it's wonderful to notice that it is a community of women—the gender much more likely to mess unity up!

Who named Obed? _____ (4:17)

It seems that our whole backdrop has flipped upside down along with our characters' lives. From the dark *days of the judges*, and famine, to the hopeful days of physical and spiritual harvest. The story is a reminder for us to encourage one another to look beyond our circumstances to the grander storyline of which we are a part. Blessing is being poured out on Ruth and Naomi by Boaz *and* their community. Even within an estrogen-heavy environment, we see goodness, grace, and blessing, without maligning, self-focused attitudes. There is no room for cattiness here. It's a beautiful encouragement for us to love redemption so much that we love it for everyone.

THE FAILURE OF COMMUNITY

We've talked a lot about names in our study. Take a look at a woman who was grafted into the line of Christ even though she made some shady sexual choices.

Read Gen 38:12–30. How does Ruth's approach to the disappointment of barrenness contrast Tamar's choices?

LET'S LOVE
REDEMPTION
SO MUCH THAT
WE LOVE IT FOR
EVERYONE.

THE RESTORATION OF COMMUNITY

Read 4:17–22.

Did You Know?

In 4:15, the community acclaims Ruth for being *more to her* [Naomi] *than seven sons*. The number seven in Scripture signifies perfection or completion. If a Hebrew family had seven sons it symbolized supreme blessing from God. (1 Sam 2:5, Job 1:2)[33]

In short, this section is a genealogy—and one of the most fascinating segments of this entire study. Of every name mentioned within the book of Ruth, one name shines out from all of the rest—*David*. In 4:15, the community prays that Obed would be her *"restorer of life."* The significance of Obed leading to the line of David is because Jesus Himself came from the line of David.[34] The prayers of God's people at the town gate for great blessing and restoration have been answered! Obed fathered Jesse who fathered David, whose line led to

Jesus. When we see the name Obed, we see God's redemption of Naomi's broken family line. When we read the name 'David', we are pointed to the Redeemer of mankind who comes from his line and adopts *us* into His family

Have you ever experienced exhausting relationship drama? Many of us do not maneuver within ideal relationships where boundaries are always respected and grace lurks around every corner. Do members of your community exemplify personality tendencies that make you cringe? Embarrass you? Leave you generally annoyed that they belong to your group? We already mentioned that in some circumstances, setting boundaries and keeping distance is necessary. (Titus 3:10, Eph 5) However, many of us wield fierce judgment upon others in full malice and pride. In Ruth, we see God prioritizing and preserving family lines, protecting weaker family members, and grafting sinful, immoral people into Christ's genealogy and kingdom. Christ bears with us and challenges us to remember that a central purpose of a Christ-filled heart is to reflect and to distribute the love of Christ. What joy and hope to know that when we don't get it perfectly right all of the time, there are scriptural examples of sinners like Rahab and Tamar who were purposefully chosen by God for inclusion into the genealogy of Christ. No one falls too far outside of God's restoration plan. We are worthy to stand with God's people, not because of our holiness but because of Christ's.

Group Discussion

What can we do practically to maintain a godly perspective and behavior when others within our community react poorly?

MEDITATION

We confess that we have harbored pride and judgment over others. Forgive and help us ambition for Your glory to manifest in the world, not our own.

Session 14

What's a 'Hesed'?

Words can be tricky. A *bear* is an animal. To *bear* up under pressure means to endure stress. Similarly, the word *love* takes on different meanings depending on where it is placed: an activity, a spouse, a friend, a parent. Today we are going to investigate a word in the story that is much richer than it appears on the surface. It emerges in Ruth 1:8, and resurges in 2:13 and 2:20.

Fill in the blanks.

> *"Then she said, 'I have found favor in your eyes, my lord, for you have comforted me and spoken _____ to your servant, though I am not one of your servants." (Ruth 2:13)*

> *"And Naomi said to her daughter-in-law, 'May he be blessed by the Lord, _____ whose has not forsaken the living or the dead!" (Ruth 2:20)*

The Hebrew translation of the word *kind* in this story is *hesed* (or *heced*), and it is used about 250 times in the Old Testament. It refers to God's *steadfast love* or *loving-kindness* that is based on a promise (or covenant). Rahab the prostitute made a *hesed* agreement with the spies to spare her family from death if she spared their lives first. The spies explained that when the Lord gave them victory in conquering the land, they would honor this *hesed* agreement.[35]

Our first glimpse of *hesed* language is in Ruth 1:8:

"But Naomi said to her two daughters-in-law, "Go, return each of you to her mother's house. May the Lord deal kindly with you, as you have dealt with the dead and with me."

To better understand God's *hesed*, let's tour some of its uses in Scripture to more fully grasp its meaning.

Below each Scripture, summarize the aspects of *hesed* love from the following verses.

"The Lord passed before him and proclaimed, "The Lord, the Lord, a God merciful and gracious, slow to anger, and abounding in steadfast love and faithfulness, keeping steadfast love for thousands, forgiving iniquity and transgression and sin, but who will by no means clear the guilty, visiting the iniquity of the fathers on the children and the children's children, to the third and the fourth generation." (Ex 34:6–7)

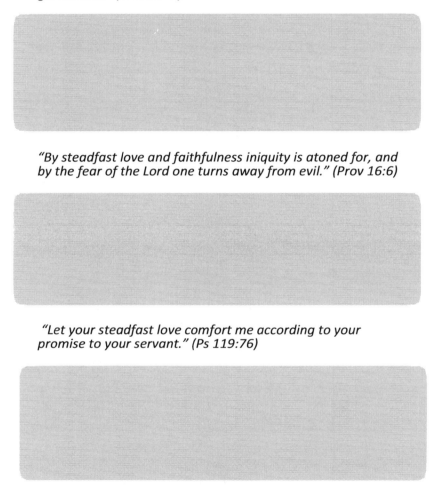

"By steadfast love and faithfulness iniquity is atoned for, and by the fear of the Lord one turns away from evil." (Prov 16:6)

"Let your steadfast love comfort me according to your promise to your servant." (Ps 119:76)

"For the mountains may depart and the hills be removed, but my steadfast love shall not depart from you, and my covenant of peace shall not be removed," says the Lord, who has compassion on you." (Is 54:10)

"Give thanks to the Lord, for he is good, for his steadfast love endures forever." (Ps 136:1)

LAWS AND GOD

The laws below are cited within the text of Ruth, and were established by God because they reflect His heart. What does each law reveal about God?

- **Levirate-Marriage (Session 4)**

- **Redemption of land (Session 4)**

- **Gleaning in the fields (Session 8)**

HESED POWER

God's laws are statements to the world about His character. When we choose to sin and break God's laws, we reject God Himself. The pressure of perfect obedience to His law was too impossible a requirement to achieve, so Jesus stepped out of heaven into human skin to fulfill the law's demands on our behalf. God looked at Christ on the cross and saw us, so now when He looks at us, He sees Christ.[36] At last, we can stand in God's presence because we were gifted with perfection that is not our own!

But God's *hesed* character goes further than replacing our condemned status with Christ's holiness—it is a rich, multi-faceted kind of love carrying a primary message of God's faithful covenant nature that's ongoing. It is also the primary overarching victory theme that rings out of Naomi's life and into our hearts today. *Hesed* love grafted Ruth into a family line not her own, and remained faithful to Naomi despite her unfaithful attitude.

You see *I am who I am* never changes.[37] Christ's *hesed* love endures when we fatigue, and is committed to us when we are unfaithful. It is an active, trustworthy love that brings security and rest to our weary souls, not only at the point of salvation, but every moment afterward. When we decided to surrender our lives to Jesus, we were in essence standing at a wedding ceremony with our Bridegroom—Christ Himself. How impossible it seems that the Author of love held our hands and spoke a sealed commitment to remain faithful to us forever, regardless of how our future sins may betray Him. His supreme, covenant character cannot fail and His seal upon our lives will not be broken. He will remain true to the promise He made to us on that day—to have and to hold us, in sickness and in health, for better and for worse, when we are faithful and faithless.[38] Behold our Bridegroom and Redeemer—Jesus Christ!

Personal Reflection

Define *hesed* in your own words.

Group Discussion

Explain the gospel (good news) about Jesus in your own words.

MEDITATION

Thank You for choosing us as Your bride despite our faithlessness! Your constant, *hesed* love gives our anxious souls rest, and generates hope in the face of despair.

What's a 'Hesed'?

Session 15

Redeeming the Darkness

Our puzzle of Ruth is complete. From three widows balling their eyes out on the side of the road, to a new marriage, baby, and legacy. Famine to harvest, multiple deaths to unexpected life, bitterness to blessing. A short little book jam packed with literary delights, a milieu of honest characters, and a profound message of a sovereign God extending *hesed* love and redemption.

Group Discussion

Take a look at the summary statements below and put a √ beside the themes that have impacted you the most in this study. Share with your group.

God allows painful circumstances to enter our lives for His purposes and glory, which can be outside of our own preferences and understanding.

God uses the prayers of His people—even when they are weak—to bless others and change events.

God has sovereign control over the world's geographic events (i.e. famine).

God foreshadowed and illustrated His plan to rescue us through Christ, using the story of Ruth.

God enjoys displaying His character through weak, ordinary people. God Himself lives in community as a member of the Trinity—He has designed us to enjoy and grow in Him by one another's influence. Other believers help keep us accountable.

God made an everlasting, unbreakable covenant with the Israelites to be their God. When they turned their hearts from Him, He remained faithful and brought them back to Himself.

God's hesed love made a commitment to us at our salvation. God will be faithful to fulfill His vow to love and cherish us regardless of our level of brokenness, and regardless of how far we've wandered away from Him.

We have glimpsed the *Sovereign* God who guides generational history and our own personal stories. God sovereignly allowed famine both geographically and emotionally. He permitted the calamity of financial impoverishment, multiple deaths, familial ruin, emotional desolation, unyielding barrenness, mental confusion, and social disrepute.

We have also encountered the *Providential* God who sustained them during their despair, and brought hope and strength when all was thought lost.

We've met a *Transforming* God who sprouted new life from the very crops that were devastated. The most shattered family line was restored to propagate the ancestry of Christ. The barren womb of ten years began to kick. The woman born into a shameful family lineage was adopted into God's family.

Our souls met the God of *hesed* love that cannot change nor fail us. He remains committed to love, empower, and redeem our current circumstances and eternal destiny because of the covenant He made to us—His bride—when we were saved.

GOD'S HESED LOVE DRIVES US FURTHER TO OUR KNEES, PLEADING FOR THE POWER AND PRESENCE OF CHRIST TO OVERCOME THE SIN THAT WE CANNOT.

As Christians, our struggle continues between our sinful nature and the life of Christ indwelling us. While we've been saved from the penalty of sin, we've not yet been saved from the presence of it. God's mercy and restoration always remain open to our return no matter what our failings have been. Those who have been forgiven much, love much. (Luke 7:47) Naomi regained her joy and her testimony, and for us, we have been grafted into the line of Christ!

The *Naomi's*, *Tamar's*, *Rahab's*, and *Me-and-You's* of the world are the exact misfits whose sin will never disqualify us from the loving arms of a pursuing Savior who refuses to let us leave. You see, His *hesed* love made a promise of betrothal to us that resounds in faithfulness, despite our constant betrayals. This does not motivate us to keep on sinning. Rather, it drives us further to our knees, pleading for the power and presence of Christ to overcome the sin that we cannot. This kind of undeserved restoration is precisely who God is by nature—a holy God who makes broken people new, and transforms dark backdrops into wings of freedom that soar across the stage.

In His time and purpose, our sovereign, providential God lifted and transformed the very famines that He permitted. We fall to our knees in reverence and submission to our God whose ways are higher than our ways (Is 55:8–9), and who is entirely good, *all* of the time. (Ps 100:5)

Personal Reflection

Skim back over your study notes from start to end and briefly summarize your most powerful take-aways below.

MEDITATION

Prepare your own Meditation today.

Leader's Guide

STARTING A BIBLE STUDY

1) Consider forming a prayer team specifically for this study. This group may arrive to meetings early to pray, pray for the group on their own, or may even consist of prayer warriors who do not attend but commit to pray anyway. Pray that hearts would respond to God's truth and that this study would speak with clarity and relevance to their individual lives.

2) Secure child care if necessary.

3) Identify people who can help facilitate discussions if your group is large or if the primary leader is unexpectedly absent. Consider rotating leaders to help train up skill in others and take the load off of one person.

4) Consider making your group intergenerational. While you may not have everything in common, the blessing of mentorship from those outside of your typical friendship circles is often worth the priority. The study is time-limited, so it is less risky to invite different personalities because you don't necessarily need to commit beyond the length of the study.

5) Ensure that all group members have books. Consider purchasing books for those who are unable to pay, for unexpected people who show up, or for newcomers as a means of welcoming them into your community.

6) Identify at the first meeting:
   - Meeting length. Start and end on time so participants feel respected.
   - Identify times and locations (church, house, rotating locations).
   - Organize snacks so that preparation of food is shared.
   - Share a meal together at some point in the study (start/mid/end). There is a relationship between building community and food!
   - Decide how many sessions to discuss at each meeting. Some groups may want to review one session per meeting, other groups two or more, others may want to vary the numbers each week.
   - Establish consensus around expectations for confidentiality. Members need to feel safe to share without fear of judgment or exposure beyond the group setting.

LEADING THE MEETING

1) For the first meeting, allow people to share about themselves. Ice breakers may be helpful, but until you get to know each personality, be cautious about asking them to participate in anything too out of the ordinary. While some personalities thrive on drama, others will feel silently crushed under the pressure. In time, it will be easier to know group personalities and target community-building questions with greater sensitivity.

2) During each meeting:
   - Consider beginning with safe, 'can't get it wrong' questions (i.e. What's your favorite food, or what is one place you'd love to travel, or describe one interesting thing that happened to you this week). It is more likely that quiet people will participate in study discussion if you get them talking out loud within the first 5–10 minutes.
   - Open in prayer. Ask the Holy Spirit to guide discussion and impact hearts. Keep re-centering conversation back to biblical truth and Jesus.
   - Share requests and pray for your participants at every meeting.

LEADER PREPARATION

1) Be prayerful about God giving you favor as you lead, for a gentle and respectful approach, for wisdom to know what to discuss and how to redirect the group if required, for connection among participants, and that God's presence would be sensed among you as a community. Remember to pray for group members outside of the meetings as well.

2) The leader may structure the meeting in several ways such as:
   - Opening and concluding the meeting with prayer.
   - Reading the portions of Ruth that are relevant to session during the meeting.
   - Have someone read various points of session commentary to help get the group unified on topic details.
   - Conclude by summarizing the session and asking the group for their thoughts on how this impacts them.
   - Leader preparation will include identifying which Personal Reflection, Group Discussion, and general questions to select from each session that you're discussing. Participants should be made aware at the start what kinds of questions will be discussed so that they have time to reflect and prepare for the meeting.
   - End each session's discussion with an open-ended question like, "Are there any other thoughts to add before we move on?" If not, conclude the meeting or move to the next session.

QUESTION SELECTION

While any questions can facilitate discussion, it is recommended that the Personal Reflection and Group Discussion questions be used as they have been designed to generate discussion and apply biblical truth to real life. Discussion that blends both types of questions often creates a nice balance.

Prior to meeting, the leader selects questions for group discussion. Some questions may generate little discussion, and this is okay! It is a good idea to select more than one or two questions from each session in the event that it is a quieter night. If not all of the selected questions are used because discussion has been particularly lively around one topic, remaining questions can be left unused or returned to at the next meeting.

Try to avoid letting conversation get stuck on one question at the expense of others. Questions that generate enthusiasm for discussion can be great if this helps group members apply biblical truth and connect with one another relationally. But lively discussion is not necessarily an indicator of fruitful discussion and can also be a time-waster if it becomes too tangential. Consider sharing the structure for discussion that you've chosen so that group members can help you stay on track for content and time. Consider identifying a timekeeper to monitor time and signal the leader when time is running short for a particular segment.

As you prepare, try choosing the same number of questions to discuss during each session, estimating an equal amount of time per question. This may help balance discussion on each topic. For example, if the meeting is 2 hours long, and 45 minutes is going to be set aside for community building, food, and prayer, then you have a remaining 1 hour and 15 minutes to discuss your chosen questions.

Finally, while these are helpful tips and tricks, there is ultimately no formula on how to lead. Don't be afraid to try different methods and use an approach that works for you and the unique needs of your group. Seek the wisdom and guidance of the Holy Spirit to lead you. Rest in the assurance that God will be faithful to direct and use the discussion to impact hearts for His glory. I have prayed much wisdom and growth for you and for special empowerment as you lead. May God richly bless your efforts for His glory.

About the Author

Andrea is a wife, mom to three great kids, and a therapist. She previously managed rehabilitation teams across one of the largest, culturally diverse regions in the province of Ontario, Canada. She was an educator, mentor, and clinician of therapeutic practice across a broad spectrum of mental, emotional, neurological, and physical health challenges.

Her Master's research focused on identifying the best ways to teach adults complex information in ways that stick and makes sense. God has used these experiences to help people recover from various kinds of brokenness, and communicate complex concepts in engaging, practical ways to diverse groups of people.

Andrea's passion has shifted toward seeing people grow in biblical literacy, and have their lives transformed by the gospel. She enjoys teaching the Bible and writes Bible studies and non-fiction Christian-living books. Her writing has been recognized by two separate national and international writing awards that seek to identify today's best upcoming Christian writers. She speaks on books of the Bible, principles found within her Bible studies, as well as relevant life issues with the perspective of how current psychological approaches intersect with biblical wisdom.

Acknowledgements

Thanks to *Write Integrity Press* for welcoming me into their writing family and supporting me prayerfully and practically in the production of this series. To Marji Laine Clubine for her conviction, enthusiasm, and diligence toward making this series a reality. To my content editor Lill Kohler for her keen eye toward shaping the final product.

Thanks to my amazing friends—too many to name—whose passion in supporting and celebrating this writing testifies to how when God calls one, He calls a community. You encouraged my pen from its infancy, rallied others to read my work, gave thoughtful advice, and prayed specific communal blessings toward this work being published. Beyond grateful.

Endnotes

1 Henry, M. (1994). Matthew Henry's commentary on the whole Bible: Complete and unabridged in one volume (372). Peabody: Hendrickson.

2 https://en.oxforddictionaries.com/definition/sojourn

3 Smith, J. E. (1995). The Books of History. Old Testament Survey Series (Ru 1:1–5). Joplin, MO: College Press.

4 Deuteronomy 23

5 Proverbs 3:5-7

6 https://en.oxforddictionaries.com/definition/bitter

7 Dockery, D. S., Butler, T. C., Church, C. L., Scott, L. L., Ellis Smith, M. A., White, J. E., & Holman Bible Publishers (Nashville, T. (1992). Holman Bible Handbook (220). Nashville, TN: Holman Bible Publishers.

8 Smith, S., & Cornwall, J. (1998). The exhaustive dictionary of Bible names (166). North Brunswick, NJ: Bridge-Logos.

9 Richards, L. O. (1991). The Bible reader's companion (electronic ed.) (175). Wheaton: Victor Books.

10 Merriam-Webster, I. (2003). Merriam-Webster's collegiate dictionary. (Eleventh ed.). Springfield, MA: Merriam-Webster, Inc.

11 Jamieson, R., Fausset, A. R., & Brown, D. (1997). Commentary Critical and Explanatory on the Whole Bible (Ru 1:1–2). Oak Harbor, WA: Logos Research Systems, Inc.

12 Biblical Studies Press. (2006). The NET Bible First Edition Notes (Ru 1:9). Biblical Studies Press.

13 Oswald Chambers, My Utmost for His Highest) Uhrichsville, OH: Barbour Publishing, Inc., 1963).

14 Richards, L. O. (1991). The Bible reader's companion (electronic ed.) (175). Wheaton: Victor Books.

15 Richards, L. O. (1991). The Bible reader's companion (electronic ed.) (175). Wheaton: Victor Books.

16 Biblical Studies Press. (2006). The NET Bible First Edition Notes (Ru 1:4). Biblical Studies Press.

17 Spurgeon, Charles. H. (2007). Morning by morning. Crossway books, Wheaton, IL.

18 Reed, J. W. (1985). Ruth. In J. F. Walvoord & R. B. Zuck (Eds.), The Bible Knowledge Commentary: An Exposition of the Scriptures (J. F. Walvoord & R. B. Zuck, Ed.) (Ru 1:16–18). Wheaton, IL: Victor Books.

19 Biblical Studies Press. (2006). The NET Bible First Edition Notes (Ru 1:4). Biblical Studies Press.

20 Biblical Studies Press. (2006). The NET Bible First Edition Notes (Ru 1:2). Biblical Studies Press.

[21]Block, D. I. (2003). Ruth, Book Of. In C. Brand, C. Draper, A. England, S. Bond, E. R. Clendenen & T. C. Butler (Eds.), Holman Illustrated Bible Dictionary (C. Brand, C. Draper, A. England, S. Bond, E. R. Clendenen & T. C. Butler, Ed.) (1422–1423). Nashville, TN: Holman Bible Publishers.

[22]Achtemeier, P. J., Harper & Row, & Society of Biblical Literature. (1985). Harper's Bible dictionary (1st ed.) (886). San Francisco: Harper & Row.

[23]https://www.inspiringquotes.us/quotes/UsfL_vDGRe3CP

[24]Biblical Studies Press. (2006). The NET Bible First Edition Notes (1 Ki 7:21). Biblical Studies Press.

[25]Richards, L. O. (1991). The Bible reader's companion (electronic ed.) (176). Wheaton: Victor Books.

[26]Biblical Studies Press. (2006). The NET Bible First Edition Notes (Ru 4:7). Biblical Studies Press.

[27]Reed, J. W. (1985). Ruth. In J. F. Walvoord & R. B. Zuck (Eds.), The Bible Knowledge Commentary: An Exposition of the Scriptures (J. F. Walvoord & R. B. Zuck, Ed.) (Ru 4:15–17). Wheaton, IL: Victor Books.

[28]Achtemeier, P. J., Harper & Row, & Society of Biblical Literature. (1985). Harper's Bible dictionary (1st ed.) (717). San Francisco: Harper & Row.

[29]Oswald Chambers. My Utmost for His Highest (Uhrichsville, OH: Barbour Publishing, Inc. 1963).

[30]Reed, J. W. (1985). Ruth. In J. F. Walvoord & R. B. Zuck (Eds.), The Bible Knowledge Commentary: An Exposition of the Scriptures (J. F. Walvoord & R. B. Zuck, Ed.) (Ru 4:11–12). Wheaton, IL: Victor Books.

[31]Dockery, D. S., Butler, T. C., Church, C. L., Scott, L. L., Ellis Smith, M. A., White, J. E., & Holman Bible Publishers (Nashville, T. (1992). Holman Bible Handbook (223). Nashville, TN: Holman Bible Publishers.

[32]Dockery, D. S., Butler, T. C., Church, C. L., Scott, L. L., Ellis Smith, M. A., White, J. E., & Holman Bible Publishers (Nashville, T. (1992). Holman Bible Handbook (223). Nashville, TN: Holman Bible Publishers.

[33]Reed, J. W. (1985). Ruth. In J. F. Walvoord & R. B. Zuck (Eds.), The Bible Knowledge Commentary: An Exposition of the Scriptures (J. F. Walvoord & R. B. Zuck, Ed.) (Ru 4:15). Wheaton, IL: Victor Books.

[34]Matthew 21:15; Rev 5:1-5

[35]Campbell, D. K. (1985). Joshua. In J. F. Walvoord & R. B. Zuck (Eds.), The Bible Knowledge Commentary: An Exposition of the Scriptures (J. F. Walvoord & R. B. Zuck, Ed.) (Jos 2:12–14). Wheaton, IL: Victor Books.

[36]2 Corinthians 5:21

[37]Exodus 3:14

[38]Ephesians 1:13

Other PNP Bible Studies

Harriet E. Michael and Shirley Crowder bless readers with the beginning of their Prayer Project.

While the project began with an in-depth study of prayers and pray-ers in both the Old and New Testaments, it quickly built to include not only a study guide that goes hand-in-hand with PRAYER, IT'S NOT ABOUT YOU, but also a thirty-day devotional called GLIMPSES OF PRAYER.

The Prayer Project has continued with their newly released PRAYER WARRIOR CONFESSIONS.

Thank you
for reading our books!

If you enjoyed this study,
please consider returning to its
Amazon page and leaving a review!

Look for other books
published by

E

Entrusted Books

an Imprint of
Write Integrity Press
www.WriteIntegrity.com

Made in the USA
Las Vegas, NV
21 December 2022

63794368R00050